project, or navigating life's daily challenges, this compact guide will help you absorb and apply Sun Tzu's strategic genius—one quote at a time.

Foreword

Deep down, you know it's time to elevate your thinking. To grow. To move with more precision, more strategy, more impact.

But the real question is: *how?*

In both warfare and business, the right strategies lead to the right tactics—and strategies always come first. No ancient text has stood the test of time more powerfully than *The Art of War* by Sun Tzu. Written over 2,500 years ago, it remains the most widely studied book on military strategy and leadership in the world.

Though originally conceived as a military treatise, Sun Tzu's wisdom has transcended time, culture, and conflict. Today, his insights are revered by political leaders, business executives, entrepreneurs, and elite performers across every field.

Once considered so powerful that it was treated as a carefully guarded state secret, the strategic principles of *The Art of War* are now freely available for anyone willing to study them. And yet, for many, reading the full text—especially for the first time—can feel overwhelming or dense.

A Strategy You Can Actually Use

This carefully curated edition—*The 200 Most Important Quotes from The Art of War*—makes it easy to absorb Sun Tzu's most essential teachings. It gives you **distilled wisdom** in a form you can **review often**, **apply quickly**, and **integrate deeply** into your thinking.

Each quote is pulled from respected translations and has been **vetted for authenticity**. Even better, the quotes are now **categorized by theme**—like Deception, Leadership, Tactics, and Timing—so you can read with focus and purpose. In just a few minutes a day, you can sharpen your mindset and rethink your strategies.

Reading the full text multiple times may be impractical for most people. But reviewing these 200 quotes regularly is not only doable—it's transformative.

How It's Helped Me

You might be wondering how these quotes can help *you*. I can best explain that by sharing how they've helped *me*.

- **I stopped talking about my plans.** I used to think sharing my ideas made me look ambitious. Now I see that it only invites resistance—or worse, someone else taking my strategy and using it first. Silence has become a strategic weapon.

- **I protect against failure before I chase success.** I used to lead with aggressive optimism. Now I think defensively first, considering weak spots before I make a final decision. It's the equivalent of securing your foundation before building the tower.

- **I study my adversaries more closely.** Sun Tzu taught me that what I *don't* know can hurt me—and what I *assume* I know can hurt me even more. I work hard to separate fact from assumption, especially when the stakes are high.

That's how it's impacted me. You'll find your own lessons as you read. But know this: **one casual pass isn't enough.** The true genius of Sun Tzu reveals itself through **frequent review and repetition**—and that's the real power of this book. It's designed for short, regular readings that deepen your understanding over time.

A Tool for Every Day

This is a book you can keep visible—on your desk, in your briefcase, on your nightstand. It's a conversation piece. A mindset reset. A personal weapon in a world of competition and complexity.

And one final thought before you begin:
While some quotes may seem similar, that's not a flaw—it's a gift. Great truths are worth hearing more than once. Each variation can trigger a new insight, depending on where you are in your journey.

You don't need to agree with every quote. You don't need to apply them all at once. But **if you reflect on them often enough**, you will begin to **think differently**… and that's when strategy becomes power.

Enjoy the journey.

Roth Stanton

Table Of Contents

UPDATED – March 2025 Edition 2

Foreword 3

Victory Without Conflict..8

Emotional Mastery & Reflection, Timing & Initiative........11

Foundational Wisdom / Core Principles.............................14

Strategy & Planning, Victory Without Conflict..................18

Deception & Psychological Warfare 21

Timing & Initiative...24

Leadership & Command, Emotional Mastery & Reflection
....27

Tactical Execution 30

Discipline & Morale 33

Terrain & Movement, & Flexibility 36

Adaptability 39

BONUS SECTION 41

   20 Quotes often inaccurately attributed to Sun Tzu's "The Art of War." 41

   10 activities Sun Tzu might have been involved with on any given day when he was alive! 45

   36 Knives / Thirty-Six Stratagems 48

   Timeline of Strategic Thought in Ancient China 53

Victory Without Conflict

Sun Tzu teaches that the highest form of victory is achieved not through open conflict, but through strategy, perception, and restraint. True mastery lies in shaping expectations, controlling the narrative, and avoiding unnecessary battles by understanding timing and opportunity. A wise leader doesn't seek war but is always prepared for it—choosing peace when possible and acting swiftly and decisively when required. Strength is not found in brute force, but in clarity, patience, and the ability to make oneself unreadable until the perfect moment to strike. In the art of war, excellence is found not in how often you fight, but in how often you win without having to.

1. Engage people with what they expect; it is what they are able to discern and confirms their projections.
2. Great generals inspire peace more than they deliver war.
3. He who wishes to fight must first count the cost.
4. If you wait by the river long enough, the bodies of your enemies will float by.
5. The greatest victory is that which requires no battle.
6. To win without fighting is the highest form of excellence.
7. When the enemy gives you an opening, be swift as a hare and he will be unable to withstand you.
8. Let your plans be as dark and impenetrable as night, and when you move, fall like a thunderbolt.

5 Affirmations for Victory Without Conflict

1. **"I strive for victory through strategy, not struggle."**
   (Inspired by 197 & 198 – the greatest triumph is the one that avoids the battlefield entirely.)

2. **"My strength lies in knowing when to act—and when not to."**
   (Inspired by 195 & 199 – wise timing and swift execution overcome any enemy.)

3. **"I master perception, letting others see only what I intend."**
   (Inspired by 193 – control begins by shaping expectations.)

4. **"Peace is my goal, but I am prepared for war—and I choose wisely between them."**
   (Inspired by 194 & 200 – a great leader aims to resolve, not destroy, but never hesitates when it's time to strike.)

5. **"I win by remaining unreadable—when I move, it is unstoppable."**
   _(Inspired by 200 – conceal your plans, then strike with decisive force.)

Emotional Mastery & Reflection, Timing & Initiative

Sun Tzu teaches that true mastery in warfare—and in life—begins with emotional discipline and strategic clarity. Anger, pride, and haste are the enemies of sound decision-making; victory belongs to those who act from calm reflection, not reactive impulse. Success comes to those who recognize when to act and when to wait, who remain fluid in the face of chaos, and who transform adversity into advantage through timing and control. Strength lies in training, preparation, and the ability to remain steady when others unravel. In every moment, clarity of purpose and emotional mastery outweigh brute force or blind aggression.

9. Anger may in time change to gladness; vexation may be succeeded by content.
10. Do not let your strategy be dictated by anger or pride.
11. He who is not courageous enough to take risks will accomplish nothing in war.
12. He will conquer who has learned the art of deviation.
13. If quick temper and recklessness dominate, defeat will follow.
14. If the mind is willing, the flesh could go on and on without many things.
15. In the midst of chaos, there is also opportunity.
16. The calmest mind can find clarity in the chaos of war.
17. The clever combatant imposes his will on the enemy but does not allow the enemy's will to be imposed on him.
18. The line between disorder and order lies in logistics.
19. Those skilled in warfare direct their forces like the turning of a stream in steep terrain.
20. Unhappy is the fate of one who tries to win battles and succeed in his attacks without cultivating the spirit of enterprise.
21. Victory usually goes to the army who has better trained officers and men.

22. When the outlook is bright, remain cautious; when the outlook is gloomy, remain hopeful.
23. Clarity of purpose is more valuable than superiority of numbers.
24. He who knows when he can fight and when he cannot will be victorious.

5 Affirmations

1: Emotional Clarity

"I release anger and pride. My strength comes from calm reflection, not reaction."
(Inspired by Quotes 41, 42, 45, 48)

Affirmation 2: Courage with Precision

"I act with boldness and patience, striking only when the time is right."
(Inspired by Quotes 43, 44, 56)

Affirmation 3: Mind Over Circumstance

"My will is stronger than my limits. In chaos, I find clarity and opportunity."
(Inspired by Quotes 46, 47, 48)

Affirmation 4: Purpose Over Pressure

"I stay focused on my mission, never letting the enemy or the moment dictate my path."
(Inspired by Quotes 49, 50, 55)

Affirmation 5: Strategy Over Struggle

"I prepare, I adapt, and I win with precision—not force."
(Inspired by Quotes 51, 52, 53, 54)

Foundational Wisdom / Core Principles

Sun Tzu's core philosophy emphasizes that true strength lies not in brute force, but in clarity, patience, and precise execution. Victory is achieved long before the battle through deliberate preparation, deception, and the ability to influence your enemy's behavior without direct confrontation. The wise commander avoids unnecessary conflict, anticipates risk, and leverages timing, terrain, and psychological advantage to create openings while concealing intent. Leadership is not measured by volume or aggression but by foresight, emotional control, and the ability to adapt quickly to change. Above all, the highest form of warfare is to subdue the enemy without fighting—through superior awareness, strategy, and the art of invisible influence.

25. A single error in judgment can lose a campaign before it begins.
26. A war won in haste may be lost in consequence.
27. Convince your enemy that he will gain very little by attacking you; this will diminish his enthusiasm.
28. Do not press a desperate enemy too hard. Leave room for retreat to prevent them from fighting to the death.
29. Even the finest sword plunged into salt water will eventually rust.
30. Even when faced with chaos, the wise general remains calm and plans clearly.
31. Force your opponent to reveal his position, then strike with certainty.
32. Fortune favors the prepared general, not the hopeful one.
33. Good generals select soldiers for their strength and assign roles according to their capabilities.
34. He who is prudent and lies in wait for an enemy who is not, will be victorious.
35. If you are far from the enemy, make him believe you are near.

36. If you know neither the enemy nor yourself, you will succumb in every battle.
37. If your strategy is transparent, your enemy will always have the upper hand.
38. In peace, prepare for war. In war, plan for peace.
39. It is only the enlightened ruler and the wise general who will use the highest intelligence of the army for the purposes of spying.
40. Leadership is a matter of foresight and balance, not just power.
41. Let your enemy underestimate you, that is your first victory.
42. Never interrupt your enemy when he is making a mistake.
43. One bold move can break the enemy's spirit more than a thousand strikes.
44. Order and disorder are a matter of organization; courage and cowardice are a matter of positioning.
45. Rewards for good service should not be deferred a single day.
46. Rouse him, and learn the principle of his activity or inactivity. Force him to reveal himself.
47. Secret operations are essential in war; upon them the army relies to make its every move.
48. Spies are a most important element in war, because on them depends an army's ability to move.
49. Strength lies not in how loudly one commands, but in how clearly one leads.
50. The best path to victory is the one your enemy does not see.
51. The difficulty of tactical maneuvering consists in turning the devious into the direct, and misfortune into gain.
52. The greatest risk is not knowing what risk you are taking.
53. The more you provoke, the more you expose.
54. The wise commander avoids conflict when victory is uncertain.
55. There are five dangerous faults which may affect a general: recklessness, cowardice, a hasty temper, a delicacy of honor, and over-solicitude for his men.

56. There is no advantage in prolonging conflict, decisive action brings peace more swiftly.
57. Those who excel in warfare subdue enemies without conflict.
58. Thus the expert in battle moves the enemy, and is not moved by him.
59. To capture the enemy's entire army is better than to destroy it.
60. To hold ground is not always to win; sometimes, retreat is the greater power.
61. Victory is not found in brute force, but in superior awareness.
62. Victory is reserved for those who are willing to pay its price.
63. Weapons are instruments of misfortune; a wise man uses them only when there is no other path.
64. When the enemy is close and remains still, he is relying on the natural strength of his position.
65. When the enemy moves rapidly, he is planning something unusual.
66. When war is inevitable, let your strategy turn necessity into opportunity.

5 Affirmations for Foundational Wisdom / Core Principles

1. **"I lead with clarity and foresight—never with haste or ego."**
   (Inspired by Quotes 151, 152 & 166 – success begins before battle, rooted in calm, deliberate preparation.)

2. **"I win not through brute strength, but through awareness, adaptability, and superior positioning."**
   (Inspired by Quotes 170, 175, 187 – the path to victory is mental and strategic.)

3. **"I let my enemy reveal himself before I move—and I strike with purpose, not impulse."**

(Inspired by Quotes 157, 172, 184 – clarity of enemy intent precedes decisive action.)

4. **"Even in peace, I prepare with wisdom; even in war, I plan with balance."**
   (Inspired by Quote 164 – strategy is timeless and always evolving.)

5. **"Victory belongs to those who dare, prepare, and remain unseen until the moment is right."**
   (Inspired by Quotes 158, 167, 176 – preparation, patience, and surprise win battles before they begin.)

Strategy & Planning, Victory Without Conflict

Sun Tzu teaches that the highest form of strategy is to win without engaging in battle at all. True mastery lies in preparation, foreknowledge, and the clarity to act only when advantage is assured. A wise commander understands both the enemy and himself, positions with care, and moves with precision—like water adapting to the shape of its surroundings. Victory is not gained by brute strength, but by subtlety, timing, and discipline. In war, as in life, success belongs to those who plan deeply, act deliberately, and choose the right moment to strike—or to wait.

67. Act after having made assessments. The one who first knows the measures of far and near wins this is the rule of armed struggle.
68. Be extremely subtle, even to the point of formlessness.
69. If quick, I survive. If not quick, I am lost. This is 'death.'
70. If your enemy is secure at all points, be prepared for him.
71. It is not the strength of the army but the clarity of the plan that wins the day.
72. Move not unless you see an advantage. Use not your troops unless there is something to be gained.
73. Position yourself where you cannot lose. Then wait for the enemy to act.
74. Security against defeat lies in the army's disposition, but the opportunity of defeating the enemy is provided by the enemy himself.
75. Strategy without tactics is the slowest route to victory. Tactics without strategy is the noise before defeat.
76. The art of war is of vital importance to the state. It is a matter of life and death, a road either to safety or to ruin.
77. The path to victory lies in knowing both the enemy and yourself.

78. The victorious strategist only seeks battle after the victory has been won, whereas he who is destined to defeat first fights and afterwards looks for victory.
79. The wise commander uses both force and guile to achieve his objectives.
80. There is no instance of a nation benefiting from prolonged warfare.
81. Those who excel in command gain their victories through planning before the battle begins.
82. To foresee a victory that the ordinary man can foresee is not the acme of skill.
83. To rely on rustics and not prepare is the greatest of crimes; to be prepared beforehand for any contingency is the greatest of virtues.
84. Ultimate excellence lies in defeating the enemy without ever having to fight.
85. Victory begins with understanding — of yourself, your enemy, and the terrain between.
86. War is a matter of vital importance to the state; a matter of life or death, the road either to survival or to ruin.
87. What enables the wise sovereign and the good general to strike and conquer, and achieve things beyond the reach of ordinary men, is foreknowledge.
88. Who wishes to fight must first count the cost.
89. A commander should be like water — adaptable and formless, seeking the path of least resistance.
90. One who sets the entire army in motion to chase an advantage will not attain it.
91. The supreme art of war is to subdue the enemy without fighting.
92. Those who win every battle are not really skillful, those who render other's armies helpless without fighting are the best of all.

5 Affirmations for Strategy, Planning & Victory Without Conflict

1. "I plan with foresight, act with precision, and seek victory before the battle begins."
   (Inspired by Quotes 93, 96, 102 – planning leads to silent triumph.)
2. "I adapt like water and strike only when the moment is right."
   (Inspired by Quotes 83, 87, 104 – fluid strategy and perfect timing.)
3. "I achieve my greatest victories not through force, but through clarity, positioning, and wisdom."
   (Inspired by Quotes 86, 88, 99, 106 – winning without fighting.)
4. "I lead with purpose, count the cost, and let discipline shape the path to success."
   (Inspired by Quotes 91, 95, 103 – responsibility in strategic leadership.)
5. "I master both strategy and tactics—knowing myself, the enemy, and the terrain makes my path inevitable."
   (Inspired by Quotes 90, 92, 100 – total awareness breeds unstoppable momentum.)

Deception & Psychological Warfare

Sun Tzu teaches that deception is the essence of strategic superiority. True victory is not found in overwhelming force, but in the ability to control perception—misleading the enemy, striking where they are weakest, and masking true intent until the decisive moment. To win without battle is the highest art, and that is only possible when you remain unreadable, unpredictable, and always one step ahead. Psychological warfare—through illusion, bait, and misdirection—breaks the enemy's will before the conflict even begins. In this way, a wise commander leads with subtlety, concealing strength behind stillness and guiding events from the shadows with precision and purpose.

93. All warfare is based on deception.
94. Attack him where he is unprepared, appear where you are not expected.
95. Confuse and divide your enemy let fear replace their focus.
96. Hold out baits to entice the enemy. Feign disorder, and crush him.
97. If the enemy knows not where he will be attacked, he must prepare in every quarter, and so be everywhere weak.
98. It is better to outwit the enemy than to outfight him.
99. Let your enemy underestimate your ambition, and you have already won half the war.
100. Let your plans be dark and impenetrable as night, and when you move, fall like a thunderbolt.
101. One must know how to appear predictable while remaining unpredictable.
102. Pretend inferiority and encourage his arrogance.
103. Reveal nothing. Hide your formation as a spider hides in its web.
104. The appearance of weakness can be a fortress if crafted with intention.
105. The whole secret lies in confusing the enemy, so that he cannot fathom our real intent.
106. War is a series of misdirection, only those who master illusion prevail.
107. War is governed by deception, and therefore before battle one must feign weakness.
108. Warfare is the Tao of deception: all truth hides behind strategy.
109. When you are strong, appear weak. When you are weak, appear strong.
110. Your strength lies not in what you reveal but in what you conceal.

111. Hence to fight and conquer in all your battles is not supreme excellence; supreme excellence consists in breaking the enemy's resistance without fighting.

5 Affirmations for Deception & Psychological Warfare

1. **"I lead with strategy, not ego—winning by design, not force."**
   (Inspired by: "All warfare is based on deception." and "It is better to outwit the enemy than to outfight him.")
2. **"I am a master of perception—I reveal only what I intend."**
   (Inspired by: "Your strength lies not in what you reveal but in what you conceal." and "Let your plans be dark and impenetrable…")
3. **"I strike from the shadows with clarity, purpose, and precision."**
   (Inspired by: "Feign disorder, and crush him." and "Fall like a thunderbolt.")
4. **"I shape outcomes by directing attention—not through confrontation, but through control."**
   (Inspired by: "Confuse and divide your enemy…" and "The whole secret lies in confusing the enemy…")
5. **"I move unseen, my strength concealed, my intentions unreadable—until the moment is mine."**
   (Inspired by: "Pretend inferiority…", "Appear where you are not expected…", and "Warfare is the Tao of deception…")

Timing & Initiative

Sun Tzu's message on timing and initiative is clear: success belongs to those who master both patience and precision. He teaches that swift action is powerful only when rooted in foresight and restraint. A wise leader knows when to move and when to wait—striking not from impulse, but from calculated advantage. Timing isn't just about speed; it's about knowing when the enemy must act and using that moment against them. In war, as in life, the path to victory is paved by anticipation, discipline, and the ability to stay still like a mountain—or move like a storm.

112. When the way is open, move like the wind. When resistance is great, stay like the mountain.
113.
114. Avoid the opponent whose spirit is strong; do not swallow bait offered by the enemy.
115. Be swift as the wind, gentle as the forest, fierce as fire, and unshakable as the mountain.

116. Concentrate your energy and hoard your strength. Wait for the right opportunity to strike.
117. He who exercises no forethought but makes light of his opponents is sure to be captured by them.
118. Speed in war is of the essence, for delay gives the enemy time to prepare.
119. Strike when the enemy must act, not when you are ready.
120. The skillful fighter puts himself into a position which makes defeat impossible.
121. The wise commander fights only battles he knows he can win.
122. Throw them into perilous situations and they will survive; plunge them into desperate straits and they will come off in safety.
123. Throw your soldiers into positions whence there is no escape, and they will prefer death to flight.
124. To anticipate is to control; to control is to win.
125. Weapons are tools of fear; a decent man uses them only when he must.
126. When the general is weak and without authority, when his orders are not clear, it is a sign of impending defeat.

5 Affirmations for Timing & Initiative

1. **"I move with the wind when the path is open and hold like the mountain when it is not."**
   (Inspired by Quote 136 – timing is balance between speed and stillness.)
2. **"I act only when the moment is mine, not when impulse calls."**
   (Inspired by Quote 143 – strike based on the enemy's need to act, not your own impatience.)
3. **"I wait patiently, gather my strength, and strike with focused force when the opportunity arises."**
   (Inspired by Quotes 140 & 142 – conserve energy and unleash it with precision.)

4. **"I do not fear danger—I know that pressure awakens strength and purpose."**
   (Inspired by Quotes 146 & 147 – adversity can create unity and courage.)
5. **"I lead with clarity, anticipate with wisdom, and never act without intention."**
   (Inspired by Quotes 145 & 148 – foresight is the foundation of victory.)

Leadership & Command, Emotional Mastery & Reflection

Sun Tzu emphasizes that true leadership is a balance of strength, wisdom, and emotional control. A commander must be alert, decisive, and grounded in clarity—not driven by pride or fear—but by the responsibility to serve and protect. Great leaders earn the trust of their soldiers through justice, benevolence, and discipline, knowing that unity and morale are as crucial as strategy. The wise general avoids unnecessary conflict, wins through preparation, and understands both the psychology of war and the human heart. Above all, leadership is not about glory—it is about foresight, restraint, and the ability to make victory inevitable before the battle begins.

127. A general must be alert and adaptive. The battlefield will not wait for indecision.

128. A general must see with clarity and act with decisiveness.
129. A general who lacks vision is a danger to his own men.
130. A good commander is benevolent and unconcerned with fame.
131. Do not engage an enemy more powerful than you. And if it is unavoidable and you do engage, ensure you divide his forces.
132. He who advances without coveting fame and retreats without fearing disgrace, whose only thought is to protect his country and do good service for his sovereign, is the jewel of the kingdom.
133. He who relies solely on warlike measures shall be exterminated; he who relies solely on peaceful measures shall perish.
134. He will win who knows when to fight and when not to fight.
135. If he is generous with rewards and punishes justly, he will gain the hearts of his men.
136. If you know the enemy and know yourself, you need not fear the result of a hundred battles.
137. Leadership is a matter of intelligence, trustworthiness, humaneness, courage, and sternness.
138. Managing many is the same as managing few. It is a matter of organization.
139. Ponder and deliberate before you make a move.
140. The commander is the arbiter of the people's fate, the man on whom it depends whether the nation shall be in peace or in peril.
141. The commander stands for the virtues of wisdom, sincerity, benevolence, courage, and strictness.
142. The commander who understands both the art of war and the psychology of men shall not be defeated.
143. The peak efficiency of knowledge and strategy is to make conflict unnecessary.
144. The skillful leader leads without arrogance, commands without cruelty, and wins without boasting.

145. The skillful leader subdues the enemy's troops without any fighting.
146. Victorious warriors win first and then go to war, while defeated warriors go to war first and then seek to win.
147. Weak leadership brings ruin even to strong armies.
148. An army that lacks unity will crumble before it ever meets the enemy.
149. An army without discipline is more dangerous to itself than to its foes.
150. A general must not only master combat but also emotion.
151. A wise general makes a point of foraging on the enemy. One cartload of the enemy's provisions is equivalent to twenty of one's own.

5 Affirmations for Leadership, Emotional Mastery & Command

1. **"I lead with clarity, wisdom, and purpose—never rushed, never uncertain."**
   (Inspired by Quotes 57, 58, 69 – decisiveness, clarity, and reflection.)
2. **"I earn trust through justice, courage, and sincere leadership."**
   (Inspired by Quotes 65, 67, 71 – emotional intelligence and virtue-based leadership.)
3. **"I win without ego and act without fear—my duty is to serve, not to boast."**
   (Inspired by Quotes 60, 62, 74 – humility and service over recognition.)
4. **"I know when to act and when to wait—true victory is knowing both."**
   (Inspired by Quotes 64, 76 – timing and control over impulse.)
5. **"I lead united, disciplined teams with vision and heart—my power lies in preparation and unity."**
   (Inspired by Quotes 68, 77, 78, 79 – organization, discipline, and morale.)

Tactical Execution

Sun Tzu's guidance on tactical execution emphasizes clarity, timing, and adaptability over brute strength or repetition. Victory favors those who strike where the enemy is weakest, adapt their tactics to the situation, and never miss an opportunity when it arises. He teaches that success comes not from mastering every technique but from deeply understanding a few, executing them with precision, and adjusting with fluidity. Foreknowledge, decisiveness, and emotional control are key—hesitation invites defeat. Most importantly, great commanders shape the battle before it begins by exploiting the enemy's vulnerabilities, guiding outcomes with subtlety and skill.

152. Begin by seizing something your opponent holds dear; then he will be amenable to your will.
153. Build your opponent a golden bridge to retreat across.
154. Do not repeat the tactics which have gained you one victory, but let your methods be regulated by the infinite variety of circumstances.

155. Energy may be likened to the bending of a crossbow; decision, to the releasing of the trigger.
156. Foreknowledge must be obtained from men who know the enemy's situation.
157. If fighting is sure to result in victory, then you must fight.
158. If the enemy leaves a door open, you must rush in.
159. In war, numbers alone confer no advantage. Do not advance relying on sheer military power.
160. Let fear take root in your enemy's heart before the first blow is struck.
161. Success in warfare comes not from learning every technique, but in mastering a few deeply.
162. Success in warfare is gained by carefully accommodating ourselves to the enemy's purpose.
163. The control of a large force is the same principle as the control of a few men: it is merely a question of dividing up their numbers.
164. The wise general avoids the strong and strikes the weak points of his enemies.
165. Those who use the military skillfully do not raise troops twice and do not transport provisions three times.
166. When the outlook is bright, bring it before their eyes; but tell them nothing when the situation is gloomy.
167. He who hesitates when the opportunity arises will regret it forever.

5 Affirmations for Tactical Execution

1. **"I strike with precision, aiming at what matters most to my opponent."**
   (Inspired by Quote 108 – seize what the enemy values to control the outcome.)
2. **"I adapt my methods to the moment, mastering flexibility over routine."**
   (Inspired by Quote 110 – success lies in variety, not repetition.)

3. **"I act swiftly when opportunity appears, knowing hesitation breeds regret."**
   (Inspired by Quote 123 – strike when the door opens.)
4. **"I prepare deeply, master key tactics, and trust in timing and insight."**
   (Inspired by Quotes 111, 117, 112 – mastery and foreknowledge enable flawless execution.)
5. **"I lead with clarity, strike the enemy's weak points, and move with confident purpose."**
   (Inspired by Quotes 120, 114, 113 – effectiveness over force, action over delay.)

Discipline & Morale

Sun Tzu teaches that discipline and morale are the foundations of a strong, united force—and they begin with the leader. Clear commands, emotional stability, and consistent enforcement foster loyalty and obedience. A wise general treats troops with humanity but also holds them accountable, earning both respect and control. Disorganization, fear, and collapse are not the fault of the soldiers, but of leaders who fail to guide with clarity and purpose. Ultimately, effective leadership means commanding with both heart and firmness, creating an army willing to follow through even the harshest trials.

168. Do not pursue an enemy who simulates flight; do not attack soldiers whose temper is keen.
169. He who commands with confidence wins the loyalty of his troops.
170. He will win who has military capacity and is not interfered with by the sovereign.
171. If orders are understood but not obeyed, it is the fault of the officers and soldiers.
172. If soldiers are punished before a personal attachment is formed, they will not submit. If not obedient, they are useless.
173. If words of command are not clear and distinct, if orders are not thoroughly understood, the general is to blame.
174. Let your soldiers be treated with humanity, but kept under control by discipline.
175. Observe their formations, test their resolve, and disrupt their rhythm.
176. Regard your soldiers as your children, and they will follow you into the deepest valleys.
177. When commands are consistently enforced, the soldiers will be obedient.
178. When one treats people with benevolence, justice, and righteousness, and reposes confidence in them, the army will be united in mind and all will be happy to serve their leaders.
179. When troops flee, are insubordinate, collapse in disorder, or are routed, it is the fault of the general.
180. A general should not be angry, nor should a soldier be afraid.

5 Affirmations for Discipline & Morale

1. **"I lead with clarity, consistency, and calm strength—my team reflects the order I create."**
   (Inspired by: Quotes 33, 37, 39 – clarity in command and responsibility for cohesion.)

2. **"Respect and discipline go hand in hand—I earn loyalty by leading with both heart and principle."**
   (Inspired by: Quotes 32, 34, 36 – the bond between leadership, respect, and obedience.)
3. **"I cultivate unity by treating others with fairness, confidence, and vision."**
   (Inspired by: Quote 38 – benevolence and confidence create unity.)
4. **"My commands are rooted in purpose, and my strength lies in my steady example."**
   (Inspired by: Quotes 29, 30, 40 – confidence in leadership and emotional composure.)
5. **"I correct with wisdom, guide with clarity, and lead with unwavering discipline."**
   (Inspired by: Quotes 31, 32, 33 – responsibility for communication and correction.)

Terrain & Movement, & Flexibility

Sun Tzu emphasizes that victory belongs to those who master movement, adaptability, and the use of terrain. Striking swiftly and unexpectedly forces the enemy into reaction, allowing the agile leader to dictate the pace and place of battle. A wise general prepares well in advance, studies the landscape, and uses both natural features and enemy behavior to create opportunity. Flexibility in movement and strategy—not brute strength—determines success. And in all maneuvers, one must never trap an enemy so tightly that desperation leads to chaos; wisdom always allows for controlled outcomes.

181. Appear at points which the enemy must hasten to defend; march swiftly to places where you are not expected.
182. Great results can be achieved with small forces when properly directed.
183. Know the enemy, know yourself; your victory will never be endangered.
184. Speed is the essence of war. Take advantage of the enemy's unpreparedness.
185. The enlightened ruler lays his plans well ahead; the good general cultivates his resources.
186. The natural formation of the country is the soldier's best ally.
187. The opportunity of defeating the enemy is provided by the enemy himself.
188. The quality of decision is like the well-timed swoop of a falcon which enables it to strike and destroy its victim.
189. When the enemy is close at hand and remains quiet, he is relying on the natural strength of his position.
190. When you penetrate deeply into a country, it is serious ground. When you penetrate but a little way, it is facile ground.
191. When you surround an army, leave an outlet free. Do not press a desperate foe too hard.
192. Do not climb heights in order to fight. So much for mountain warfare.

5 Affirmations for Terrain, Movement & Flexibility

1. **"I move with speed, strike where I'm not expected, and force the enemy to chase my shadow."**
   (Inspired by Quote 124 – use surprise and speed to control momentum.)
2. **"I do more with less by aligning direction with purpose."**
   (Inspired by Quote 125 – small forces can win when guided wisely.)

3. **"I prepare early, observe terrain, and let the land work in my favor."**
   (Inspired by Quotes 128 & 129 – preparation and natural advantages win battles.)
4. **"I remain flexible, adjusting to every shift in position, pressure, and timing."**
   (Inspired by Quotes 130 & 131 – timing and adaptability conquer strength.)
5. **"I give space to desperation, knowing that overwhelming pressure without wisdom invites chaos."**
   (Inspired by Quote 134 – always leave an outlet when surrounding an enemy.)

Adaptability

Sun Tzu teaches that adaptability is the foundation of lasting strength in conflict. Rather than rigidly clashing with power, success lies in flowing around resistance and exploiting the weak, the overlooked, and the undefended. War is fluid by nature, and those who hold to fixed strategies will be broken by unexpected change. The greatest leaders move with clarity, adjust in real time, and close the gap between intention and action with speed and precision. Just as water shapes itself to any vessel, a wise strategist reshapes their plan to meet the moment—and that is how victory is secured.

193. Adaptation is the key to survival in battle.
194. Avoid what is strong. Attack what is weak.
195. Let your strategy be formless, then your enemies cannot prepare against it.
196. Strike at the chasm between strategy and execution, that is where armies fall.
197. The best generals are those who can adapt to changing circumstances and remain fluid like water.
198. The nature of war is constant change.
199. You can be sure of succeeding in your attacks if you only attack places which are undefended.
200. A divided army is a defeated army.

5 Affirmations for Adaptability & Flexibility

1. **"I thrive in change and adjust my strategy with clarity and confidence."**
   (Inspired by: "Adaptation is the key to survival in battle.")
2. **"I focus my energy where resistance is low and opportunity is high."**
   (Inspired by: "Avoid what is strong. Attack what is weak.")

3. **"My strategy is fluid, evolving, and impossible to predict."**
   (Inspired by: "Let your strategy be formless…" and "The nature of war is constant change.")
4. **"I close the gap between vision and execution with precision and agility."**
   _(Inspired by: "Strike at the chasm between strategy and execution…")
5. **"Like water, I flow around obstacles and break through where I am least expected."**
   _(Inspired by: "The best generals are those who can adapt…" and "You can be sure of succeeding…")

BONUS SECTION

20 Quotes often inaccurately attributed to Sun Tzu's "The Art of War."

1. "Plan for what is difficult while it is easy. Do what is great while it is small."

Anticipate trouble before it arises — mirrors his emphasis on preparation and foresight.

2. "Opportunities multiply as they are seized."

This is about momentum — seizing initiative, which parallels his view that speed and timing win battles. the quote.

"Opportunities multiply as they are seized" is not an original quote from Sun Tzu's "The Art Of War."

While the sentiment of being proactive and taking advantage of opportunities aligns with the general strategic thinking found in "The Art Of War," this specific phrasing is not present in the text.

This quote is more commonly attributed to various modern motivational speakers and business leaders. It reflects a principle of taking action to create further possibilities, which is a widely applicable concept but not a direct excerpt from Sun Tzu's work. Therefore, while the idea of seizing opportunities is implicitly present in Sun Tzu's strategies, this particular quote is a more contemporary expression of that idea.

3. "The wise warrior avoids the battle."

Often quoted in business circles. It echoes The Art of War's theme: supreme excellence is breaking the enemy without fighting — though this exact line doesn't appear.

4. "To know the road ahead, ask those coming back."

A proverb attributed to Eastern philosophy, it emphasizes the value of intelligence — a central theme in Sun Tzu's thinking.

5. "A leader leads by example, not by force."

Attributed to Lao Tzu but aligned with Sun Tzu's indirect approach. Influence beats control.

6. "Move swift as the wind and closely-formed as the wood. Attack like the fire and be still as the mountain."

Sounds like Sun Tzu — this comes from later interpretations and paraphrased lines inspired by his imagery.

7. "Victory comes from finding opportunities in problems."

Modernized paraphrasing of a deeper idea in Eastern strategy: where there is crisis, there is also potential.

8. "A good commander is benevolent, wise, and courageous."

This line comes from later military texts influenced by Confucian ethics, but reflects ideals Sun Tzu valued.

9. "The greatest weapon is the enemy's mind.

This summary reflects his obsession with deception, morale, and intelligence — though not an exact quote.

10. "Disorder came from order; cowardice came from courage; weakness came from strength."

Attributed to Wei Liaozi, a contemporary military thinker. Resonates with Sun Tzu's philosophy of dynamic balance.

11. "Control your soldiers as you would control your own children."
A Confucian-infused idea appearing in later military commentaries. Leadership is parental, not punitive.

12. "A general must be calm in crisis, firm in danger, and cautious in success."
Pulled from Six Secret Teachings (another ancient Chinese military text). Complements Sun Tzu's stress on emotional control.

13. "First win the trust of the people, then win the war."
This strategic-social idea came from Eastern governance philosophy and is echoed in later Han dynasty war writings.

14. "If you want to control the enemy, let him control himself."
A Taoist-style twist on misdirection and psychological warfare.

15. "Those who know do not speak. Those who speak do not know."
From Lao Tzu's Tao Te Ching. A sharp contrast to war-room culture — but a spiritual echo of strategic silence.

16. "He who prepares quietly for war is already feared."
A proverb derived from Chinese oral tradition, fitting Sun Tzu's preference for unseen strength.

17. "When the water is too pure, no fish can live."
From Zhuangzi. A poetic metaphor for overly rigid systems — suggesting flexibility is superior, like Sun Tzu's "formlessness."

18. "The more you sweat in peace, the less you bleed in war."
Attributed to a Chinese proverb, it echoes Sun Tzu's emphasis on preparation and drilling before conflict.

19. "A plan violently executed now is better than a perfect plan next week."

Often misattributed to Sun Tzu, this line is closer to Patton — but fits well in a discussion of timing vs. perfection.

20. "The battle is won before it is fought."

One of the most common misattributed quotes — it paraphrases Sun Tzu's broader idea but never appears as written.

10 activities Sun Tzu might have been involved with on any given day when he was alive!

It's important to remember that historical details about Sun Tzu's daily life are scarce and largely based on legend and inference from "The Art of War." However, we can make educated guesses about activities he might have been involved in on any given day:

1. **Studying Military Strategy and History:** As a renowned strategist, Sun Tzu likely dedicated time to researching past battles, analyzing military doctrines, and refining his own theories on warfare. This would involve reading scrolls, discussing tactics with advisors, and perhaps even studying terrain maps.

2. **Advising a Ruler or Warlord:** If employed, a significant portion of his day would involve consulting with his patron on military matters. This could include strategizing for upcoming campaigns, analyzing enemy movements, and offering advice on troop deployment and logistics.

3. **Teaching and Mentoring Disciples:** It's plausible that Sun Tzu had students or junior officers whom he instructed in the principles of his military philosophy. This might involve lectures, discussions, and practical exercises (though the latter is less documented).

4. **Writing and Refining "The Art of War":** The creation of his seminal work would have been an ongoing process. He might have spent time writing down his thoughts, organizing his principles, and refining his language to ensure clarity and impact.

5. **Observing Troop Training and Exercises:** To ensure the practical application of his theories, Sun Tzu might have observed military training exercises, offering feedback and making adjustments to improve the effectiveness of the troops.

6. **Scouting and Intelligence Gathering:** Depending on his role and the current military situation, Sun Tzu might have been involved in gathering intelligence about potential adversaries. This could involve sending out scouts, analyzing reports, and assessing the strengths and weaknesses of opposing forces.

7. **Planning Logistics and Resource Management:** A successful military campaign relies heavily on logistics. Sun Tzu might have been involved in planning the supply of food, weapons, and other resources necessary for an army.

8. **Engaging in Diplomatic Efforts (Indirectly):** While "The Art of War" emphasizes strategy over direct conflict, Sun Tzu likely understood the importance of diplomacy. He might have advised rulers on strategies to avoid war or to weaken enemies through alliances and political maneuvering.

9. **Reflecting on Current Affairs and Political Landscape:** A keen understanding of the political climate was crucial for a strategist. Sun Tzu would likely have spent time analyzing the relationships between different states and the potential for conflict or alliance.

10. **Personal Study and Contemplation:** Beyond military matters, Sun Tzu might have engaged in personal study of philosophy, history, or other subjects to

broaden his understanding of the world and inform his strategic thinking. He might have also spent time in quiet contemplation to develop his insights.

It's important to reiterate that these are informed possibilities. The actual daily life of Sun Tzu remains largely a mystery, adding to the mystique surrounding this influential figure.

36 Knives / Thirty-Six Stratagems

Sharp Lessons in Strategy, Deception, and Psychological Insight

"Where *The Art of War* gives you the map, the 36 Stratagems show you the trapdoor."

The "36 Knives" are drawn from a collection of ancient Chinese military stratagems known as the Thirty-Six Stratagems—a compilation of tactical and psychological principles that trace their roots to Chinese warfare, diplomacy, and statecraft. Though not directly linked to *The Art of War* by Sun Tzu, they share a cultural and intellectual lineage grounded in centuries of strategic thinking. These stratagems are sharp, subtle, and often ruthless—designed not just for battlefield victories, but for winning without fighting, manipulating perception, and destabilizing opponents from within.

Unlike traditional warfare manuals focused on force and movement, the 36 Knives blend tactical agility with strategic cunning. They reveal a mindset that values indirect pressure, psychological disarray, and exploiting human behavior as much as terrain or numbers. Understanding them is not about adopting deception as a default, but about recognizing the tools, tricks, and traps that a clever adversary might employ.

They are included here not as endorsements, but as illustrations—to expose the edges of competitive thinking, and to sharpen your awareness of how conflict, power, and perception can be manipulated by those willing to operate in the shadows. Use this knowledge not to deceive, but to defend. Not to dominate, but to discern. These are not lessons in ethics—they are insights into mindset.

Carry them as you would a knife: with care, with clarity, and with respect for the damage they can do.

I. Winning Stratagems (Advantage in a Superior Position)

1. **Deceive the heavens to cross the sea** (瞒天过海) – Mask your true goals with an ordinary act.

2. **Besiege Wei to rescue Zhao** (围魏救赵) – Attack an enemy's weak point to force a retreat.

3. **Kill with a borrowed knife** (借刀杀人) – Use another's strength to defeat your enemy.

4. **Wait at leisure while the enemy labors** (以逸待劳) – Rest and prepare while your enemy is exhausted.

5. **Loot a burning house** (趁火打劫) – Exploit a situation when your enemy is in crisis.

6. **Make a sound in the east, then strike in the west** (声东击西) – Mislead and surprise.

II. Enemy Engagement (Dealing with Stronger Opponents)

7. **Create something from nothing** (无中生有) – Deceive with illusion or misinformation.

8. **Openly repair the gallery roads, but sneak through the passage of Chencang** (明修栈道，暗度陈仓) – Create a false trail, then strike from an unexpected route.

9. **Watch the fire from the other side of the river** (隔岸观火) – Observe and wait for the right moment to act.

10. **Hide a dagger behind a smile** (笑里藏刀) – Appear friendly while plotting harm.

11. **Sacrifice the plum tree to preserve the peach tree** (李代桃僵) – Let go of the lesser to save the greater.

12. **Take the opportunity to pilfer a goat** (顺手牵羊) – Take advantage of small opportunities as they arise.

III. Attack Stratagems (Engage and Disrupt)

13. **Beat the grass to startle the snake** (打草惊蛇) – Provoke a reaction to expose the enemy's position.

14. **Raise a corpse from the dead** (借尸还魂) – Revive old ideas or traditions to serve new purposes.

15. **Lure the tiger off the mountain** (调虎离山) – Draw an enemy out of a stronghold.

16. **Let the enemy off in order to catch him later** (欲擒故纵) – Release an enemy temporarily to set a trap.

17. **Throw out a brick to attract jade** (抛砖引玉) – Offer something minor to gain something valuable.

18. **Catch the leader to capture the band** (擒贼擒王) – Target the leader to collapse the whole.

IV. Mixed Strategy (Confuse & Manipulate)

19. **Remove the firewood from under the pot** (釜底抽薪) – Undermine the source of your enemy's strength.

20. **Disturb the water to catch a fish** (混水摸鱼) – Exploit chaos for personal gain.

21. **Slough off the cicada's golden shell** (金蝉脱壳) – Escape under disguise or with misdirection.

22. **Shut the door to catch the thief** (关门捉贼) – Trap your enemy before attacking.

23. **Befriend a distant state while attacking a neighbor** (远交近攻) – Secure alliances while weakening local rivals.

24. **Borrow a safe passage to conquer the kingdom of Guo** (假道伐虢) – Use a temporary alliance for long-term gain.

V. Confrontation Stratagems (Adversity & Chaos)

25. **Replace the beams with rotten timbers** (偷梁换柱) – Sabotage or replace from within.

26. **Point at the mulberry but curse the locust** (指桑骂槐) – Indirectly criticize to avoid confrontation.

27. **Feign ignorance without losing advantage** (假痴不癫) – Appear foolish to hide your true intentions.

28. **Let the enemy tire himself out while conserving energy** (上屋抽梯) – Trap the enemy after luring him in.

29. **Deck the tree with false blossoms** (树上开花) – Mislead with illusions of success or strength.

30. **Make the guest act as the host** (反客为主) – Invert power dynamics and seize control.

VI. Desperate Stratagems (For Use in Extreme Situations)

31. **Use beauty to ensnare** (美人计) – Distract with seduction or temptation.

32. **Use an empty fort strategy** (空城计) – Bluff strength when you are weak.

33. **Let the enemy's own spies sow discord in the enemy camp** (反间计) – Turn spies or insiders against the enemy.

34. **Inflict injury on oneself to win the enemy's trust** (苦肉计) – Sacrifice yourself to gain credibility.

35. **Chain stratagems together** (连环计) – Combine strategies for complex deception.

36. **Run away to fight another day** (走为上计) – In dire situations, retreat is the best option.

Timeline of Strategic Thought in Ancient China

The Cultural Context Behind the 36 Stratagems

Spring and Autumn Period (770–476 BCE)

- **Rise of Strategic Philosophy**
  - China is divided into many feudal states, constantly at war.
  - Thinkers like **Confucius** and **Laozi** begin shaping Chinese thought.
  - Warfare is brutal and frequent—ideas of cunning and diplomacy grow in parallel with brute force.

Warring States Period (475–221 BCE)

- **Birth of Strategic Texts**
  - The famous **Seven Military Classics** begin to emerge.
  - **Sun Tzu's** *The Art of War* is written (~500 BCE), focusing on deception, flexibility, and victory without conflict.
  - Stratagems and psychological warfare become formalized tactics.
  - Generals begin using spies, misinformation, and terrain like tools in a kit.

Qin Dynasty (221–206 BCE)

- **Unification & Centralized Power**

- Under **Qin Shi Huang**, China is unified for the first time.
- Strategies of manipulation and swift dominance are systematized.
- Massive walls, roads, and armies represent both power and paranoia.

Three Kingdoms Period (220–280 CE)

- **Tactical Brilliance in Practice**
  - Legendary generals like **Zhuge Liang** use clever stratagems in real battle (e.g., *Empty Fort Strategy*).
  - Many of the 36 stratagems are later attributed to this chaotic, brilliant era.

Southern & Northern Dynasties to Tang Dynasty (420–907 CE)

- **Compilation Begins**
  - The **Thirty-Six Stratagems** begin to take form as a coherent set.
  - They are passed down orally, through folklore and military tales.
  - Widely referenced in civil disputes, court intrigue, and warfare.

Ming & Qing Dynasties (1368–1912)

- **Text Solidified**
  - The Thirty-Six Stratagems are formally written down as a concise, poetic list of strategic rules.

- Their tone is sharper than *The Art of War*, more Machiavellian, focused on deception, manipulation, and survival.

20th Century to Today

- **Reintroduced & Globalized**
  - Rediscovered by scholars and used in military, business, and even **modern psychological warfare**.
  - Frequently quoted in Chinese military academies, boardrooms, and even political strategy.
  - Studied globally for their insight into **unconventional tactics and psychological leverage**.

The Complete Guide To Sun Tzu's "The Art Of War"

Beyond the Text: The Most Comprehensive Guide to *The Art of War* — A fully <u>immersive</u> <u>experience</u> with deep analysis, historical comparisons, and stunning visuals.

Amazon Link: <u>https://www.amazon.com/dp/B0F1DQ1C88</u>

The Ultimate *Art of War* Companion: A Complete Breakdown of Strategy, Leadership, and Warfare — More than just a book, this is a masterclass in Sun Tzu's philosophy.

What Makes This Book A Complete Immersive Experience / Guide To *The Art Of War*?

- **60+ Stunning <u>BLACK</u> & <u>WHITE</u> Images & Illustrations** — Experience Sun Tzu's strategies like never before with vivid, high-quality visuals designed to deepen your understanding. *A print book is an investment in clarity, insight, and your own mastery of The Art of War.*

- **Deep-Dive Analysis of All 13 Chapters** — Breaking down Sun Tzu's wisdom for modern readers, including **245 DIRECT QUOTES** broken down by chapter. (**The Art of Wisdom: Unlocking Sun Tzu's Genius Through Quotes.**)

- **Detailed Side-by-Side Comparisons of Sun Tzu With 20 Legendary Military Leaders** — *The Art of War* strategies and tactics compared with Napoleon, Attila the Hun, Genghis Khan, and 17 more. (**Sun Tzu** vs. The Titans of War: Where Theory Meets Reality).

- **A Deep Comparative Analysis of Sun Tzu Vs. The Discourses Of:**
    - Niccolò Machiavelli
    - Carl von Clausewitz
    - Miyamoto Musashi: The Book of Five Rings

- **Translations & Interpretations Compared** – The author's perspective on Thomas Cleary, Lionel Giles, Ralph Sawyer, Denma, and more, highlighting their differences, strengths, and how they shape our understanding of Sun Tzu's wisdom.

- **Modern Applications & Case Studies** – How Sun Tzu's strategies apply to business, leadership, competition, and personal success today.

- **12 Weapons That Changed War:** The Evolution of Warfare including the Impact of drones on Modern Warfare Strategies

- **The Art of War for the 22nd Century** – How *The Art of War* may evolve in the digital age and may evolve in the NEXT 100 YEARS

- **AI: Is It the Next Superweapon? -** How artificial intelligence is reshaping strategy in warfare and business.

- **An In-Depth Look at The Three Words That Define Sun Tzu's Genius: "STRATEGY OVER FORCE"** – The Core of Sun Tzu's Wisdom and Its Influence on Power, War, and Leadership

- **The Ultimate Immersive Experience** – A complete, multi-dimensional study of *The Art of War* like never before!

The Art of War Like You've Never Seen It Before

THIS IS NOT JUST ANOTHER TRANSLATION OR SURFACE-LEVEL COMMENTARY, THIS IS *THE ART OF WAR* COMPLETELY ILLUMINATED (WITHOUT HAVING TO READ THE TRANSLATIONS OF THE TEXT SEVERAL TIMES TO GRASP THEIR FULL MEANING).

Through immersive visuals, in-depth analysis, and real-world applications, this book makes Sun Tzu's wisdom more relevant than ever. Whether you're a military historian, business leader, strategist, or simply fascinated by the power of timeless knowledge, this is the *definitive guide* you've been searching for.

Reading a translation of *The Art of War* is valuable, but true **understanding** requires deeper context. Go beyond translation with **deep analysis, historical comparisons, and modern applications**. Featuring **245 direct quotes, strategic insights from 20 legendary military leaders, and stunning visuals**, this book offers the **ultimate immersive experience** for mastering Sun Tzu's wisdom.

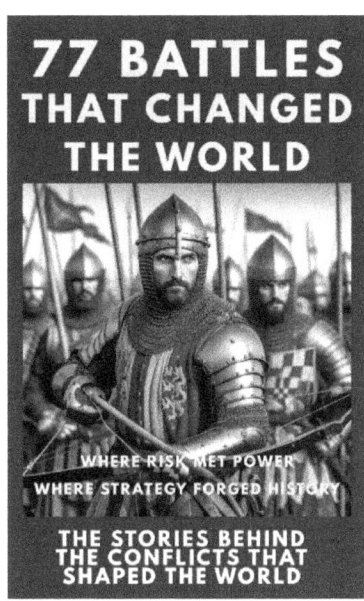

77 Battles That Changed the World is a powerful, accessible guide to the most pivotal conflicts in human history, each one presented in a **fast, focused, and visually compelling format** designed for modern readers.

History doesn't just live in dusty textbooks, it lives in moments of tension, defiance, and brilliance that shaped the world we know today.

Amazon Link:
https://www.amazon.com/dp/B0F69XNB7W

Each of the 85+ chapters is written to be absorbed quickly, whether you have 10 minutes on a coffee break or just want to learn something before bed. And you don't need to read them in order, every entry stands on its own, delivering powerful insights in a single sitting.

What's inside every chapter:

- A quick yet vivid breakdown of **what happened, who was involved, and why it mattered**
- A clear picture of **the commanders, empires, ideologies, or nations** on both sides
- A concise recap of **the top 3 lessons or takeaways** from each battle
- Over **90 images and illustrations** to bring the history to life

Why this book matters: In an age of global uncertainty, understanding the roots of conflict, and the forces that shaped today's political and cultural landscapes, is not just fascinating. It's empowering.

This book offers a crash course in **geopolitical literacy**, ideal for anyone who wants to:

- Feel confident in **conversations about world affairs or historical parallels**
- Understand the **strategic mindsets of leaders, rebels, and empires**
- Recognize the patterns that **still echo in headlines today**

Whether you're a history buff, a lifelong learner, or just someone who wants to be **"educated without the lecture"**, this book gives you the clarity, context, and confidence to connect the dots.

Here is a partial list of the Table Of Contents (85 Chapters)
SECTION 1: NO WAY BUT FORWARD – COMMITMENT, SACRIFICE, AND THE WILL TO ENDURE
Chapter 1: Burn the Ships (Cortez) – commitment without retreat
Chapter 2: 300 Spartans at Thermopylae – valor at the gates
Chapter 3: The Alamo – fighting to the last man
Chapter 5: The Kamikaze Pilots – when belief becomes a bomb
SECTION 2: MIND OVER MUSCLE - STRATEGY, SURPRISE, DECEPTION & INTELLIGENCE
Chapter 13: The Trojan Horse – deception as a weapon
Chapter 18: The Navajo Code Talkers – language as a weapon

SECTION 3: THE UNLIKELY VICTORS - UNDERDOGS WHO OUTSMARTED POWER / / WHERE SMALLER FORCES, WEAKER ARMIES, OR OVERLOOKED LEADERS PULLED OFF GREATNESS

Chapter 34: David and Goliath – small, fast, smart:

Chapter 35: The Battle of Isandlwana – when spears shattered empire

Chapter 36: Zulu at Rorke's Drift – when 150 hold back 4,000

SECTION 4: LEADERSHIP & LEGACY - TITANS AT THE CROSSROADS – COMMANDERS, CLASHES, AND CRITICAL

Chapter 45: Julius Caesar Crossing the Rubicon - irrevocable leadership moves

Chapter 46: Alexander the Great's Campaigns - momentum and bold vision

Chapter 49: The Battle of Waterloo - the end of an era

SECTION 5: REVOLUTIONS & RESISTANCE / / WHEN PEOPLE RISE – REBELLIONS, REVOLUTIONS & RESISTANCE UPRISINGS

Chapter 73: The Haitian Revolution – when slaves became a nation

Chapter 74: The American Revolution - when ideas took up arms

Chapter 75: The French Revolution - when the people toppled a crown

SECTION 6: FAULT LINES OF FURY: WARS RESHAPING THE WORLD TODAY

Chapter 82: The Enduring Shadow: A Brief History and Analysis of the Ukraine-Russia Conflict

Chapter 83: A Century of Struggle: A Brief History and Analysis of the Israel-Palestinian Conflict

Chapter 84: The Unfinished Civil War: A Brief History and

Analysis of the China-Taiwan Tension

Chapter 85: 10 Additional Significant World Hotspots And Ongoing Conflicts That Have Substantial Effects On International Relations.

EPILOGUE – 10 UNIVERSAL LESSONS FROM HISTORY'S STRATEGIC CODE

Stoic Meditations: The Legends And Lessons: Master Self-Discipline, Emotional Control, and Success, The Stoic Way

What if the key to mental strength has been waiting for you for 2,000 years?

USED BY EMPERORS. BUILT FOR YOU!

STOIC MASTERY STARTS HERE.

Amazon Link:
https://www.amazon.com/dp/B0F4MP855K

In a world of stress, distraction, and emotional overwhelm, Stoicism offers something rare: clarity, calm, and control.

This isn't just philosophy. It's a blueprint for inner power.

Stoic Meditations: The Legends and Lessons brings the lives and lessons of Zeno, Seneca, Epictetus, and Marcus Aurelius into the modern world, and into your hands.

Inside, You'll Discover:

- The true stories of the ancient Stoics, how they lived, what they endured, and why their wisdom survives

- Modern-day examples, from George Washington to Viktor Frankl and Admiral Stockdale

- Daily practices to sharpen your focus and master your emotions

- Mental tools to lead yourself and others with integrity and resolve
- A **30-Day Stoic Challenge** to help you put wisdom into action, every day

THIS BOOK WON'T JUST MOTIVATE YOU. IT WILL *STRENGTHEN* YOU.

For Readers Who Are Ready To:

- • Stop reacting and start thinking
- • Stop chasing and start leading
- • Stop consuming noise and start building inner clarity
- • Live with courage, calm, and conviction

Why Readers Love This Book:

- "This book isn't just wise , it's *usable*."
- "A modern guide to living like the greats."
- "It's made me stronger , at work, at home, and in my head."

Whether you're leading a business, a family, or just yourself, this book will help you rise.

Your discipline. Your focus. Your life. It begins now , the Stoic way.

THINK LIKE MARCUS. ACT LIKE EPICTETUS. LIVE LIKE YOU MEAN IT.

History doesn't just live in dusty textbooks, it lives in moments of tension, defiance, and brilliance that shaped the world we know today.

AI Is Calling : Master AI In 30 Easy-To-Understand Lessons That Turn Confusion Into Clarity Kindle Edition

THE SMARTEST $20 YOU WILL INVEST ALL YEAR!

Amazon Link: https://www.amazon.com/dp/B0FM8HR76Y

Being Part of the AI Conversation Matters!

You don't need to become a prompt wizard, chatbot builder, or AI agent engineer overnight…

But you *do* need to be *conversational*… fast.

Because the moment your boss, client, or competitor brings up AI, your response either positions you as *future-ready*…

Or *frozen in 2023*.

Table Of Contents

Why This Book Is Exactly What You Need to Master AI, Fast

50 Ways To Put AI Power in Your Hands & Turn AI Confusion Into Clarity & And Exactly Where to Find Them

How To Get The Most Out Of This Book

SECTION I: The AI Upheaval - Why Yesterday's Rules Won't Survive Tomorrow

Introduction: "The Inevitable Storm"

Chapter 1: The Collapse of Job Security - Why Traditional Roles Are Disappearing, And What Comes Next for Knowledge Workers

Chapter 2: Credentials vs. Competence - Why AI Values Skills Over Diplomas, and How to Stay Relevant

Chapter 3: The Broken Career Path - How AI is Rewriting

Advancement, and How to Build Your Own Ladder

Chapter 4: Automation at the Gates - AI Agents Are Replacing Roles Faster Than You Think

Chapter 5: UNFAIR ADVANTAGE: Use AI to Leapfrog Your Peers and Future-Proof Your Career

Chapter 6: Business Owners - Don't Hire New Employees, Train Existing Employees on AI

SECTION II - YOUR 30-DAY AI BLITZ COURSE

Lesson 1 - Understanding the "Text-To" Revolution: Turning Words Into Everything

Lesson 2 - LLM -Large Language Models; The Sum Of All Knowledge

Lesson 3: Training Your AI; what It Means, Why It Matters, How To Do It

Lesson 4: The Ultimate Prompt Model; Expert Prompt Engineering, INSTANTLY

Lesson 5: AI-Powered Search –Your Superpower To Find Anything, Summarize Everything… Instantly (The World's Knowledge At Your Fingertips)

Lesson 6: Generative AI: The Framework for Creation and Innovation

Lesson 7: Text-to-Text AI: Turns Words Into Workflows, Content, And Strategy

Lesson 8: Text-to-Image AI: Create Stunning Visuals From Words

Lesson 9: Text-to-Video AI: Transform Text Into Professional Videos

Lesson 10: Text-to-Speech AI: Type Words; Hear Perfect Voices

Lesson 11: Text-to-Music AI: Generate Extraordinary Songs From Simple Prompts

Lesson 12: Text-to-3D AI – Build Virtual Worlds With Words

Lesson 13: Text-to-Document AI: Generate Polished Documents Effortlessly... In Minutes
Lesson 14: Text-to-Code AI: Build Software With Words
Lesson 15: Organizing Your Data for AI Success: From Chaos to Clarity
Lesson 16: Tech Stacking – The Tools That 10X You
Lesson 17: Chatbots – Your 24/7 Digital Assistant
Lesson 18: AI Agents – Your Autonomous Digital Workforce
Lesson 19: Autonomous Workflows – Orchestrating Your Digital Operations
Lesson 20: No-Code AI – Build Million-Dollar Solutions Without Writing a Single Line of Code
Lesson 21: Prompting AI to Build Your Perfect Step-By-Step Playbooks
Lesson 22: Building Websites, Landing Pages, and Marketing Funnels with AI
Lesson 23: Building Complete Brands from Scratch with AI
Lesson 24: Writing All Your Sales Copy and Email Campaigns with AI
Lesson 25: Creating and Editing High-Converting Videos with AI
Lesson 26: Running Your Calendar, Booking Calls, and Managing Outreach with AI
Lesson 27: Mapping Your AI-Driven Customer Journey
Lesson 28: Cloning Yourself: Building Your Digital Twin with AI: Be Everywhere All At Once
Lesson 29: Putting It All Together, 10 Real Use Cases, 10 AI Wins
Lesson 30: AI Governance & Sample Company Use Policy

Tariffs Explained for Business Leaders: Everything You Need to Know About the World's Most Misunderstood Trade Tool Kindle Edition

Amazon Link:

https://www.amazon.com/dp/B0F446YT4M

In today's unpredictable global economy, **tariffs have gone from background noise to boardroom priority.** Whether you're leading a multinational operation, scaling a startup, or simply navigating rising costs, tariffs can affect everything from pricing and profitability to public perception.

This isn't a textbook—it's a practical playbook.

Written for decision-makers, not economists, this comprehensive guide breaks down what tariffs *really* are, how they work, and how to strategically respond. It's loaded with real-world examples, business risks and opportunities, and proven tools to help you future-proof your organization in a volatile world.

Table Of Contents
Author's Note: Tariffs in Turbulent Times / As of August 8, 2025
The Triple Helix: How Tariffs, Regulations, and Policy Interweave to Shape Global Commerce
INTRODUCTION
PART I – Understanding Tariffs: What Every Leader Needs to Know
CHAPTER 1: What Is a Tariff, Really?
CHAPTER 2: Why Governments Use Tariffs

CHAPTER 3: How Tariffs Actually Work
CHAPTER 4: Who Pays for Tariffs?

PART II – Case Studies in Conflict: How Tariffs Disrupt and Reshape Markets

CHAPTER 5: The Strategic Use of Tariffs in Government Policy
CHAPTER 6: Tariffs as Economic Weapons
CHAPTER 7: Industries Most Commonly Targeted in Trade Wars
CHAPTER 8: Business Risks Tariffs Create
CHAPTER 9: Business Opportunities from Tariffs
CHAPTER 10: How to Read and React to Tariff Policy
CHAPTER 11: Lessons from Emerging Economies

PART III – Tools for Tariff Resilience: Strategic Planning & Leadership

CHAPTER 12: The Tariff Impact Matrix
CHAPTER 13: Building a Tariff-Resilient Supply Chain
CHAPTER 14: Navigating Public Relations & Communication During Tariff Crises

PART IV – What Comes Next: Forecasting the Tariff Era

CHAPTER 15: The Future of Tariffs — and How to Lead Through What's Coming
CHAPTER 16: Tariffs, Automation, and AI
CHAPTER 17: Digital Tariffs & Global Tech
CHAPTER 18: Digital Tax & Tariff Landscape Around the World
CHAPTER 19: Conclusion: What Business Leaders Must Know Now

PART V – BONUS CONTENT

CHAPTER 20: Breakdown – Who Really Pays the Tariff?
CHAPTER 21: Tariff Impact on Global Supply Chains
CHAPTER 22: Quick Reference Guide: 10 Questions to Ask Before Entering a Tariff-Exposed Market

CHAPTER 23: Tariff Policy Timeline: Key Moments That Shaped Global Trade
CHAPTER 24: Smoot-Hawley and the Great Depression: What It Did — and Didn't — Cause. And Why It Still Matters Today.
CHAPTER 25: Smoot-Hawley Tariff Timeline – The Policy That Shook Global Trade
CHAPTER 26: The Post-War Trade System - From Bretton Woods to the WTO: The Age of Liberalized Trade
CHAPTER 27: Tariffs in the 21st Century - China, Trump, and the New Nationalism
CHAPTER 28: A Timeline of 21st-Century Tariff Flashpoints
CHAPTER 29: Tariff-Proofing Your Business
CHAPTER 30: Case Study: The U.S.–China Trade War
CHAPTER 31: Case Study: Steel & Aluminum Tariffs
CHAPTER 32: Case Study: The Auto Industry & USMCA
Glossary of Trade Terms

ADDENDUM:

"Liberation Day" Tariffs: A Deep Dive Into President Trump's Tariff Era

A Comprehensive Analysis of Trade Policy (January 2025 – August 11, 2025)

The U.S.-China Trade Confrontation: A Central Conflict - Updated Analysis Through August 11, 2025

The U.S.-Canada Trade Confrontation: A Bilateral Crisis Analysis - Updated Analysis Through August 11, 2025

The U.S.-Mexico Trade Relationship: Navigating Tariffs and Diplomacy - Analysis Through August 11, 2025

The U.S.-UK-EU Trade Triangle: Navigating the New Tariff Architecture - Analysis Through August 11, 2025

THE AUTHORITY BOOK FORMULA
How to Publish a Book That INSTANTLY Makes You the GO-TO NAME in Your Field

What if one book could change the entire trajectory of your career?

In a marketplace buried under endless social posts, podcasts, and flashy ads, authority is the new currency. And nothing builds unshakable authority faster than a **strategic book with your name on the cover.**

Amazon Link: https://www.amazon.com/dp/B0FMP5R1ST

Your book isn't just words on a page — it's a **trust shortcut.** It's the proof that positions you as the **go-to name in your field**, elevates your influence, and magnetizes opportunities that others chase for years.

Inside *The Authority Book Formula*, you'll discover:

✅ **Why a book outperforms every other platform** — social posts vanish, ads eat your budget, but a book pays dividends for years.
✅ **The Trust Shortcut effect** — how your book collapses years of networking and branding into a single credibility move.
✅ **How to shift from "best-kept secret" to "category leader"** — and stop competing on price.
✅ **The Five Pillars of an Authority Book** — exactly what makes the difference between a forgettable book and the one people call their "industry Bible."
✅ **The 90-Day Post-Launch Playbook** — how to turn your

book into leads, media invitations, and paid speaking gigs.

✅ **Authority multipliers** — the system for turning one book into keynotes, masterminds, press features, and a reputation that outpaces competitors.

Who This Book Is For

- **Coaches & consultants** ready to attract high-ticket clients.

- **Executives & entrepreneurs** who want to lock in credibility and influence.

- **Creators & experts** looking for the fastest way to command attention in a noisy market.

Whether you want to dominate your niche, land speaking engagements, or be seen as the **undisputed leader in your field**, your book is the master key.

Don't just write a book. Write the book that makes you unforgettable.

The Authority Book Formula is your blueprint for building industry-shaping influence, turning your ideas into impact, and claiming your rightful place as the trusted thought leader your clients, peers, and audiences are already waiting for.

Best wishes for continued success!

P.S. If you found this book helpful, I'd be truly grateful if you could take just a minute to share your thoughts with others.

Your honest review on Amazon (or wherever you purchased the book) makes a huge difference — it not only helps new readers decide if this book is right for them, but it also allows me to keep creating resources that serve professionals like you.

I know your time is valuable, so even a short review — just a sentence or two about what you found most useful — would mean a great deal.

Thank you for being part of this journey toward a better understanding and application of "Sun Tzu's "The Art Of War."

With gratitude,
Walt

Content Nexus Publishing specializes in creating engaging, high-quality books that educate, entertain, and inspire readers across diverse topics, including fiction, non-fiction, & puzzles.

Content Nexus Business & Leadership Library